I SEE COLOR

An Affirmation and Celebration of Our Diverse World

written by **Valerie Bolling** and **Kailei Pew**

illustrated by **Laylie Frazier**

HARPER

An Imprint of HarperCollinsPublishers

For all children. I see you and your beautiful color.
Your color is part of who you are, but it's not only what you are.
Be proud of all that you are and will become.
—V.B.

For children everywhere. You are beautiful, powerful, and strong.
May you always see and be seen completely.
—K.P.

To my family. Mom, Dad, Chanelle, Shaina, Kailyn, Tamir,
and Bun–I hope you find yourselves reflected in these pages.
And to Jess, Annie, and Jet. Thank you for the support you provided
me during the most difficult parts of this artistic endeavor.
—L.F.

I See Color
Text copyright © 2024 by Valerie Bolling and Kailei Pew
Illustrations copyright © 2024 by Laylie Frazier
All rights reserved. Manufactured in Italy.
No part of this book may be used or reproduced in any manner whatsoever without written
permission except in the case of brief quotations embodied in critical articles and reviews.
For information address HarperCollins Children's Books, a division of HarperCollins
Publishers, 195 Broadway, New York, NY 10007.
www.harpercollinschildrens.com
Library of Congress Control Number: 2023940811
ISBN 978-0-06-323426-0

The artist used Procreate on a 2020 iPad Pro to create the digital illustrations for this book.
Typography by Rachel Zegar
24 25 26 27 28   RTLO   10 9 8 7 6 5 4 3 2 1
First Edition

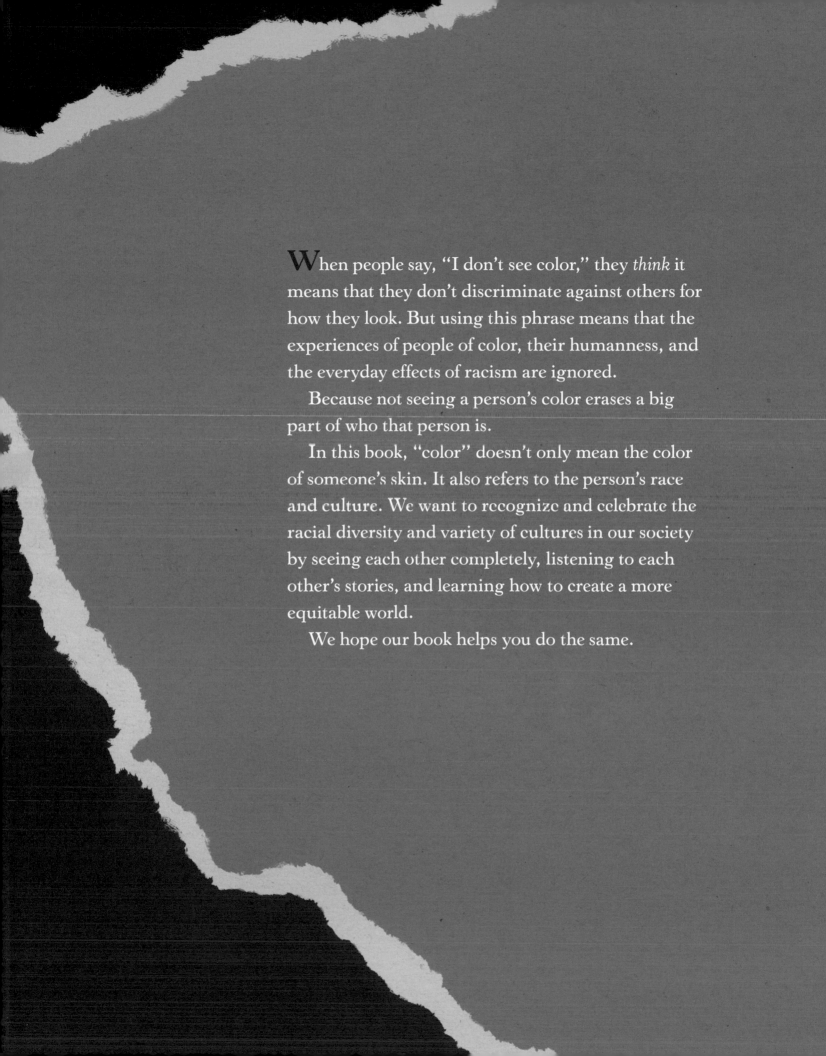

When people say, "I don't see color," they *think* it means that they don't discriminate against others for how they look. But using this phrase means that the experiences of people of color, their humanness, and the everyday effects of racism are ignored.

Because not seeing a person's color erases a big part of who that person is.

In this book, "color" doesn't only mean the color of someone's skin. It also refers to the person's race and culture. We want to recognize and celebrate the racial diversity and variety of cultures in our society by seeing each other completely, listening to each other's stories, and learning how to create a more equitable world.

We hope our book helps you do the same.

Cool like an autumn breeze.
Warm like the summer sun.
Steady like the night.
Rising like the dawn.
Beautiful like a quilt of
stitched-together stories.

I see color.

and standing up for those words until people listened.

Elizabeth and Roy Peratrovich

I see **WARM BEIGE**, striking against poor working conditions and demanding higher pay.

Sue Ko Lee

And **POWDERED OAK**,
rising up against bias,
defying injustice,
and refusing to
be silenced.

Fred Korematsu

Leading to **SOFT SUEDE**, linking different groups together to accomplish one goal.

Yuji Ichioka and Emma Gee

I see **GLEAMING STARDUST**, defending precious Native land and preserving a sacred heritage.

Madonna Thunder Hawk and Tom Goldtooth

With them, **RICH SEPIA**, protecting cherished resources and honoring Mother Earth.

I see **COOL AMBER**, reaping newfound rewards for those who silently sowed.

Dolores Huerta and Cesar Chavez

17th Street
Elementary School

Sylvia Mendez

And there, **RADIANT BRONZE**, opening school
doors and proving that separate is not equal.

I see **DEEP UMBER** and **TAWNY BROWN**, using their
words to shed light, spread love, and speak for a movement.

PEACE. FAITH. LO

JUSTICE.

UNDERSTANDING

Dr. Martin Luther King Jr.

Malcolm X

A movement of **EBONY, SIENNA, BLUSH,** and **CEDAR,** sparking necessary change.

Top row: John Lewis, Jesse Jackson, A. Philip Randolph, Marva Collins, and Barbara Jordan

Bottom row: Cicely Tyson, Fannie Lou Hamer, Adam Clayton Powell Jr., and Shirley Chisholm

Inspiring a new Black movement of
MAHOGANY, BRASS, and **HICKORY . . .**
because change still needs to come.

Ayo Tometi, Alicia Garza, and Patrisse Cullors

I see **IVORY**, listening more than they speak and standing as true allies.

Anne and Carl Braden

And **ALABASTER ROSE**, moving forward
from tragedy with empathy and understanding.

Rabbi Abraham Joshua Heschel

I see **GOLDEN EMBERS**, reminding us of a nation forgotten.
Lifting their voices for a people remembered.

Native Hawaiian Protesters and Haunani-Kay Trask

Dr. Ahmad Jaber

Then **CREAMY PEARL**, speaking truth when others chose fear, and advocating for We the People.

Basemah Atweh

Now I see a **FULL PALETTE**.

Individually, distinct, like the sound of each voice.

In unison, a powerful chorus, celebrating all that can be achieved together.

NOT LEFT, NOT RI
FORWARD
ENDRACISM
Defend Dreamers!
#CITIZENSHIP FOR ALL
STOP ASIAN HATE
BLACK LIVES MATTER

I listen to the songs and learn their stories.

I see color.

I love color.

Don't you?

AUTHORS' NOTES

I've often had people tell me they don't see my color. When people say that, they usually mean that they don't see my race—that my race doesn't matter. Yet, my race *does* matter. It's an important part of who I am. So when someone says they don't see my color, then they don't truly see me, and that's hurtful.

Children, it's okay to admit that you see someone's color, especially if it's different from your own. What you shouldn't do is make assumptions or judgments about people based on the color of their skin or their race or culture. You should get to know people and listen to and learn from their stories.

When you are open to listening to people's stories and learning from their experiences, you'll discover that people are sometimes treated poorly because of the color of their skin or race. Sometimes people with lighter skin are treated better than those with darker skin. And that's wrong.

So what can you do? You can be like the people in this book who stood up for what was right. If you see or hear someone treat another person badly because of the color of their skin or race—or for any other reason—you can speak out against it. Even if you don't make big moves like the people in this book did, remember that even small gestures matter. You can make sure your friend group includes people from different backgrounds and races. You can call out the bad behavior, comfort someone who's had a mean comment tossed at them, or reach out to those who have been excluded.

Let's see our different and beautiful colors while appreciating and celebrating them. Our world is better when everyone is treated with respect, valued, and feels a sense of belonging. That's the world the people in this book have been fighting for. Isn't that the world we all want and deserve to live in?

—Valerie Bolling

When people say, "I don't see color" in reference to the race of others, it hurts my heart every time. What they're likely trying to say is that they will treat everyone equally. But what they are actually saying is that they won't see someone completely.

A better approach is to see the color, love the color, and never discriminate against others based on their race or the color of their skin.

But just *seeing* people's color isn't enough. We also need to be better about knowing each other's stories. Growing up, I always learned about Reverend Dr. Martin Luther King Jr. in school (as I absolutely should have). But I didn't learn about most of the other people highlighted in this book. Knowing Dr. King's *and* others' stories will bring more love and acceptance into our relationships, and ultimately greater understanding to our nation and world.

I recognize that this book does not even begin to cover the many people who could have been included, but I hope you'll now go forward and learn more about them and others who have fought for change, taken a stand, or listened and acted as true allies.

Teaming up with Valerie and Laylie for this project was a dream. In coming together, we hope to show what can happen when people from different backgrounds unite to make a difference.

While racism is still a big problem today, we can actively fight against it. We can listen to and learn from those around us who have different experiences. We can speak up when we see injustice. We can advocate for much-needed change.

Let's notice each other's beautiful colors. Let's listen to each other's specific stories. Let's see each other completely.

—Kailei Pew

PEOPLE AND MOVEMENTS TO SEE

ELIZABETH PERATROVICH (1911–1958) AND
ROY PERATROVICH (1908–1989)

Elizabeth and Roy Peratrovich were the grand presidents of the Alaska Native Brotherhood and Alaska Native Sisterhood civil rights groups. After being excluded from "white only" public spaces and denied the chance to buy a home, they drafted a law to end racial discrimination in Alaska. At first, the bill failed. So they traveled all over Alaska, educating and petitioning government officials. Their united efforts and Mrs. Peratrovich's speech before the Alaskan Congress eventually led to the passing of the United States' very first anti-discrimination law.

SUE KO LEE (1910–1996)

After enduring sweatshop conditions and anti-Chinese discrimination as a buttonhole machine operator for National Dollar Stores, Sue Ko Lee led a strike against the factory in San Francisco's Chinatown. It was the first time Chinese workers organized as the Chinese Ladies' Garment Workers Union. The strike lasted more than three months. The union ultimately won a pay raise, more reasonable hours, and a cleaner working environment.

FRED KOREMATSU (1919–2005)

Fred Korematsu refused to enter the Japanese incarceration camps set up by the American government following the bombing of Pearl Harbor. The federal government arrested him for not complying, tried him before a judge, and ultimately sent him to a camp. Korematsu fought the case but lost. Many years after Korematsu's release, a team of attorneys helped him reopen the case, and he eventually won. He went on to lobby for legislation that admitted the systemic racism behind the camps. Thanks to his efforts, each Japanese American who had been incarcerated received twenty thousand dollars in reparations. Korematsu was one of four individuals who had similar cases, including Gordon Hirabayashi, Minoru Yasui, and Mitsuye Endo.

YUJI ICHIOKA (1936–2002)

Yuji Ichioka had experienced deep racism as a child in a Japanese incarceration camp. But it didn't end when he was released. Seeing continued discrimination and mistreatment, Ichioka wanted to unite different Asian ethnic groups to fight for change. He and his partner, Emma Gee, created the Asian American Political Alliance, which was the first time the term "Asian American" had been used. Uniting people of various Asian cultures brought much-needed attention to their activism and helped to eliminate broad, degrading terms.

MADONNA THUNDER HAWK (BORN 1940)

Madonna Thunder Hawk, a member of the Oohenumpa band of the Cheyenne River Sioux Tribe, was a leader in the American Indian Movement. The group formed to combat discrimination, reclaim Native identity and pride, and fight against the US federal government's attempt to force Native people to leave their reservations and assimilate into "modern society." Thunder Hawk created the We Will Remember Survival School, a type of home school that often took place outdoors and focused on important cultural lessons. Thunder Hawk continues to fight for Native women and children's rights today.

TOM GOLDTOOTH (BORN 1953)

Tom Goldtooth, a member of the Dine and Dakota tribes, was a leader in the environmental justice movement. He worked with other Indigenous leaders to influence climate decisions on a global level, always seeking to honor Mother Earth. He went on to become the executive director of the Indigenous Environmental Network. In 2015, he received the Gandhi Peace Award for his work.

DOLORES HUERTA (BORN 1930) AND
CESAR CHAVEZ (1927–1993)

Experienced activists Dolores Huerta and Cesar Chavez joined forces and worked together for more than thirty years as labor leaders and community organizers. After watching the terrible mistreatment of migrant workers, many of whom were Latine or from other minority groups, Huerta and Chavez cofounded the National Farm Workers Association. They organized hunger strikes, boycotts, and rallies to fight for equal pay, better working conditions, and respect for migrant farmers.

SYLVIA MENDEZ (BORN 1936)

Sylvia Mendez and her brothers, Jerome and Gonzalo Jr., were turned away from the nearby "white-only" Westminster public school in 1943 because of their darker skin and Mexican Puerto Rican heritage. They were forced to attend a run-down Mexican American school far from their home. Their father, Gonzalo, gathered other Latin American families to combat the racism and challenge the practice in court. The Mendez family were among the first Americans to successfully win an elementary school desegregation case. Their work paved the way for national school desegregation in the landmark 1945 case, *Brown v. Board of Education of Topeka*.

DR. MARTIN LUTHER KING JR. (1929–1968) AND MALCOLM X (1925–1965)

Dr. Martin Luther King Jr. and Malcolm X were prominent leaders in the civil rights movement. They both relentlessly championed the rights of Black people. While they often held different viewpoints, both fought tirelessly for racial justice. Both gave action-inspiring speeches calling for reform and became mouthpieces for the movement. And, ultimately, both lost their lives when they were assassinated for their views. The two men met only once, during the debate over what would become the Civil Rights Act of 1964.

THE CIVIL RIGHTS MOVEMENT AND THE BLACK FREEDOM STRUGGLE (1950s–1960s ERA)

The civil rights movement was a struggle for racial justice and equal treatment under the law during a time of severe discrimination against African Americans. The Black freedom struggle included work for equality in education, politics and government, film, and more. Many people came forward to advocate for change, including John Lewis, Jesse Jackson, Fannie Lou Hamer, A. Philip Randolph, Shirley Chisholm, Barbara Jordan, Marva Collins, Adam Clayton Powell Jr., and Cicely Tyson. It's important to note that the civil rights movement was sparked by resistance that began as early as the 1800s. Activists like Sojourner Truth, Ida B. Wells, and W. E. B. Du Bois had set a firm foundation for these activists of the '50s and beyond.

BLACK LIVES MATTER LEADERS (EST. 2013)

After continued racism, police brutality, persistent economic inequality, violence, and overall mistreatment of Black people, more change and reform were needed. Standing on the shoulders of the civil rights leaders who came before, new leaders rose. Alicia Garza, Patrisse Cullors, and Ayo Tometi cofounded the Black Lives Matter Global Network as part of the larger movement for Black lives. Millions of individuals joined them to advocate for needed change.

ANNE BRADEN (1924–2006) AND CARL BRADEN (1914–1975)

Anne and Carl Braden were allies who stood up for desegregation and equality during the civil rights movement. When Charlotte and Andrew Wade could not buy a home where they wanted to because of racism against African Americans, the Bradens bought it for them, even though it meant they endured violence and jail time. Mrs. Braden later cofounded the Kentucky Alliance Against Racial and Political Repression to fight against white supremacy and to promote antiracism.

RABBI ABRAHAM JOSHUA HESCHEL (1907–1972)

Rabbi Abraham Joshua Heschel finished his schooling and rabbinic ordination in Germany, only weeks after Hitler came to power. He was soon arrested by the gestapo and deported for his Jewish beliefs and activism. As the Holocaust raged, Rabbi Heschel immigrated to the United States. There, he tried to help his family to safety, but tragically, his mother and three of his four sisters were killed by the Nazis. Rabbi Heschel turned to continued activism, publicly teaching love and acceptance for all people. He knew that Jewish Americans and African Americans could band together in their efforts. He himself became a friend and ally to Dr. Martin Luther King Jr., participating in and defending the civil rights movement.

NATIVE HAWAIIAN PROTESTERS— APOLOGY RESOLUTION (1993)

The goals of the Native Hawaiian people are diverse and wide-ranging. For over one hundred years, there was no acknowledgment of the role the US government played in overthrowing the Kingdom of Hawaii. Protests brought attention to the plight of the Native people of Hawaii until Congress passed the 1993 Apology Resolution, which President Bill Clinton then signed into law. Some believe this is a good start to much-needed repairs between the US and the Native Hawaiian people.

HAUNANI-KAY TRASK (1949–2021)

Haunani-Kay Trask was a Native Hawaiian activist, poet, and educational leader who advocated for Hawaiian sovereignty and helped create the field of Hawaiian studies. She highlighted the essential need to include Indigenous voices and experiences in conversations about reparations for Native people. She passionately organized for human rights, gender equality, and Indigenous self-determination in her own islands and in other countries around the world.

DR. AHMAD JABER (1947–2020) AND BASEMAH ATWEH (1956–2005)

Dr. Ahmad Jaber and Basemah Atweh cofounded the Arab American Association of New York to help Arab immigrants with education, health care, and other social services. Following the attacks of 9/11, the association expanded to respond to the hate crimes that targeted Arab Americans and to educate others on Arab cultures.